ART ADVENTURES SERIES

BOOK 4

BASIC CRAFTS

by

Sandra M. Zawadzki

illustrated by Gary Mohrmann

Cover by Sandra M. Zawadzki

Copyright © Good Apple, Inc., 1985

ISBN No. 0-86653-301-X

Printing No. 98765432

GOOD APPLE, INC.
BOX 299
CARTHAGE, IL 62321-0299

ACKNOWLEDGEMENT

I am grateful to Jean Everingham for the help she has given me, her encouragement, and her professional advice in the development of this book. My husband, Felix, deserves a special thanks for his support and belief in my work. I also wish to extend my appreciation to Sam Newlon for his patient help.

Sincerely,

TABLE OF CONTENTS

INTRODUCTION

Art Adventures in Basic Crafts is a collection of easy-to-make projects for beginners. No longer will the busy teacher be forced to hunt through stacks of books and magazines to find suitable things for students to make. Even though the projects are intended for beginners, they vary in length and difficulty to allow flexibility in planning for a specific block of time and range of ability in a class. For the child who finishes early, additional suggestions for things to make and do appear in Additional Things to Do.

Art Adventures in Basic Crafts is fun to teach. It capitalizes on children's natural curiosity and desire to experiment. The children learn to combine color, shape and texture with natural and manmade materials. Teacher and children share in planning projects; then children create their own objects.

Needed materials are listed at the beginning of each project. Instructions are given in easy-to-follow steps with simple drawings illustrating the process. Helpful suggestions and patterns are included. A teacher is shown what to expect.

Creativity, not perfection, is the goal here. Satisfaction that comes from making something is the important consideration. Children should have the satisfaction of making something themselves with a little help, but as little criticism as possible. Too much criticism destroys incentive.

Art Adventures in Basic Crafts will be a pleasure to teach and fun for the children. . . create and enjoy the results.

MOVABLE JACKS

COLLECT. . .

Scissors
Drawing paper
String
Paper fasteners
Glue
Heavyweight 9″ × 12″ oaktag
Pencils
Acrylic paints or magic markers
Medium soft hair brushes
Compasses

STEP-BY-STEP DIRECTIONS. . .

1. Draw the main body of a simple shape lightly in pencil on heavyweight oaktag. Then draw one arm and one leg separately on remaining portion of sheet. Keep size in proportion to the body. Shoes, trousers, and hands should be drawn on the limbs. Repeat process for other appendages.

2. Decorate one, or both sides of figure with paint or magic marker, or combination.

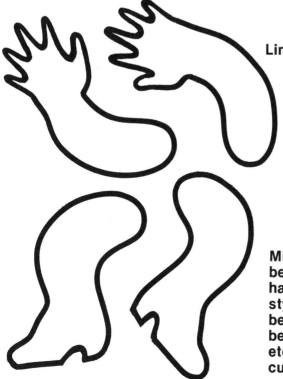

Limbs for Jack

Mitten shapes may be substituted for hands; sneakers or stylized shoes may be used; shirts may be ruffled, sweaters, etc., pants may be cuffed or not.

Body for Jack

1

3. Carefully cut out figures and limbs.

4. Make two marks close together on each limb, not too close to the edge or too far down. One hole is for the paper fastener, and one is for the string so figure can move. Puncture marks with compass point.

5. Attach limbs to body on back side with paper fasteners, using hole farthest from edge.

6. Knot-tie string and secure with glue to prevent it from coming untied, through an arm. Then take string, leaving a little slack, from the arm and slip it through the hole of the opposite arm. Knot-tie string and secure it with a dab of glue. Repeat process for legs.

7. Knot-tie and secure with a dab of glue a 10″ length of string to the center of connected arms; knot "arm" string to center of string connecting the lower legs and secure with glue. Allow 5″ or 6″ of string to hang below figure. Knot-tie and secure with glue a 2″ or 3″ length of string to head and hang to display. Pull lower string to make Jack move. Puncture a hole in center of head, tie cord, and hang to display.

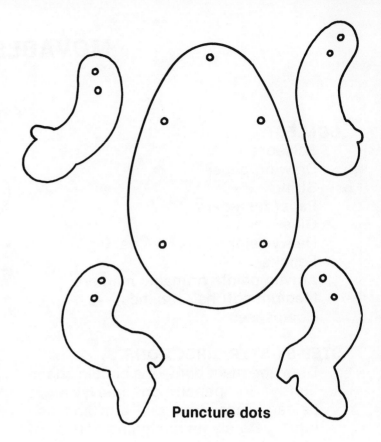

Puncture dots

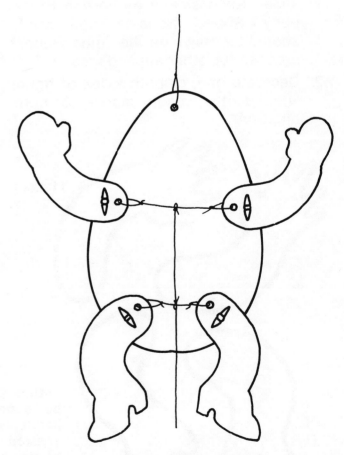

Back side

2

PAPER TREES

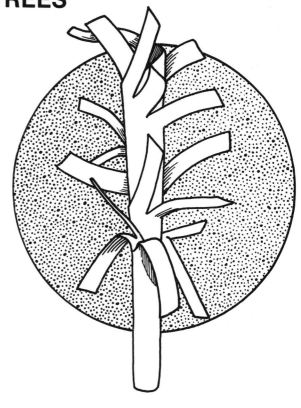

COLLECT. . .

Newspapers or 12″ × 24″ wide plain paper

2″ long pieces of tape (3 or 4 pieces per child)

Spray paint

Scissors

Glue

1½″

1½″

Cut

Cut

Cut

STEP-BY-STEP DIRECTIONS. . .

1. To make tree: Roll paper into 1½″ diameter tube. Tape roll at top, middle and bottom.

2. Make three 4″ downward cuts with scissors. Bend strips over pencil.

3. Carefully pull out center coils from the top as far as you can without pulling the roll apart.

4. Paint tree.

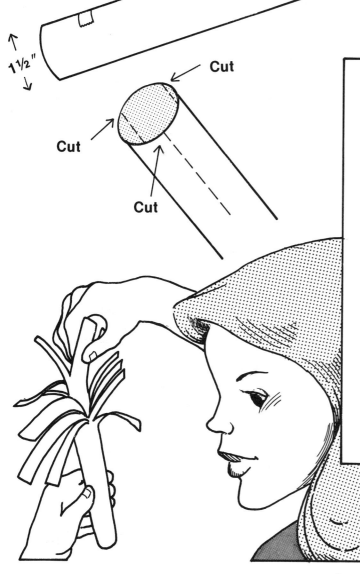

NAPKIN OR LETTER HOLDER

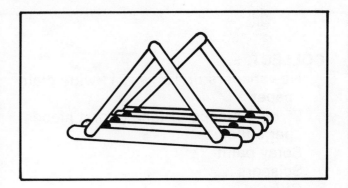

COLLECT. . .
Small Popsicle sticks
Large Indian love beads (available at art and craft supply stores)
Acrylic paint and gloss spray varnish
Glue

STEP-BY-STEP DIRECTIONS. . .

1. Paint all Popsicle sticks and spray with gloss varnish.

2. Glue an Indian love bead ½" from each end of a stick. Glue another stick to bead in same position. Repeat until you have five sticks aligned. Keep ends and sides even.

3. Form two "V" shapes by gluing two sticks together at one end.

4. Glue "V" to each side of base ½" from end.

5. Letters, napkins, or miscellaneous items can be put in the center. Shapes may be changed. See illustrations.

Add thermometer, note pad or calendar by gluing to cork to give versatility.

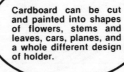

Cardboard can be cut and painted into shapes of flowers, stems and leaves, cars, planes, and a whole different design of holder.

4

A GLIDING WE GO

COLLECT...
- 8½″ x 11″ drawing or plain notebook paper
- Scissors
- Pencil, crayons
- Paper clips or fasteners (2 per child)

Let's have some fun. See who can make his glider glide the farthest.

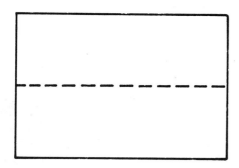

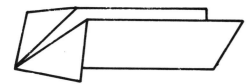

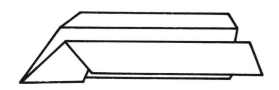

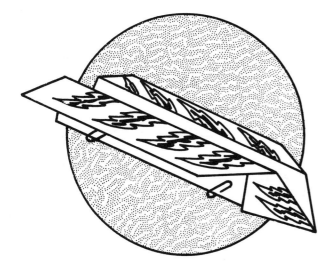

STEP-BY-STEP DIRECTIONS...

1. To make wings: Fold paper lengthwise in half. Hold paper, with unfolded edge away from you; fold both corners: one toward you and the other away from you.

2. Fold half of paper toward you and the other half away from you.

3. Decorate glider with crayon patterns.

4. Fasten two paper clips or fasteners at the bottom of folded edge or into the lower half.

TOOTHPICKING

COLLECT. . .
Round and flat toothpicks
Medium weight cardboard scraps
Glue, quick drying or white

STEP-BY-STEP DIRECTIONS. . .
1. Let children experiment with flat and round toothpicks and quick drying or white glue. Let pieces dry before making additions.
2. Cut picks with scissors or break by hand.
3. Attach creation to medium weight cardboard.

A few toothpicking ideas. Just pick your brain.

TOOLED DESIGNS

COLLECT...

    Drawing paper
    Pencils
    Black, medium-point magic marker
    1½″ nails with heads
    Mallets or hammers
    6″ × 8″ wooden blocks
    Aluminum, copper, or brass tooling
      metal (available at art and craft
      supply houses)
    Lace, ribbon, or yarn
    Large-eyed, blunt-point sewing
      needles
    Glue
    Compass
    Scissors

TEACHER PREPARATION...

Cut metal into assorted sizes with scissors—minimum: 2″ × 3″, maximum: 4″ x 7″. Cut drawing paper 1″ larger than metal size. Mimeograph designs for tooling. See next page.

STEP-BY-STEP DIRECTIONS...

1. First make a drawing of a design. Designs should be simple with few details, such as plants, animals, or objects.

2. Draw design in pencil on paper; when finished, make dots 1/8″ apart with magic marker over the drawing. This will be where the nail is hammered into metal.

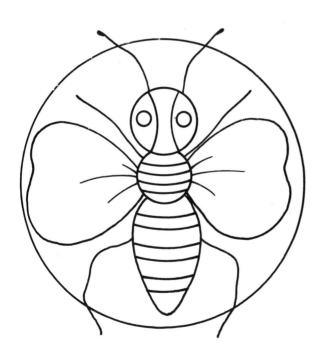

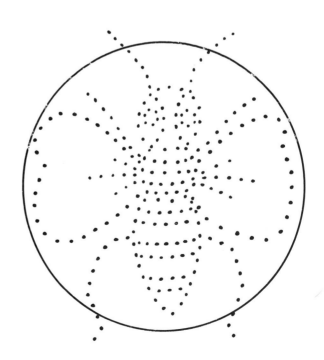

3. Tape pattern to metal and to wooden board, and hammer into the block. Check periodically to see if all the dots are being hammered. When finished, remove pattern; use guide once to avoid missing dots if pattern is punched with holes.

4. Trim edges by gluing ribbon and lace, or doing a blanket or running stitch (see illustrations) with the large blunt-pointed needle and yarn. Holes may be prepunched with compass 1/8″ apart to receive needle.

5. Knot 4″ thread to hang tooled work for display. Picture hangers and frames may also be used.

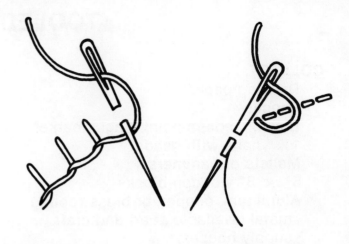

blanket
Work from left to right. Bring needle up through pattern line. Hold thread with left thumb; insert needle to right of starting point slightly above line. Bring needle below line and draw it over loop.

running
Work from right to left. Stitches must be evenly sized and spaced.

DESIGNS TO MIMEOGRAPH

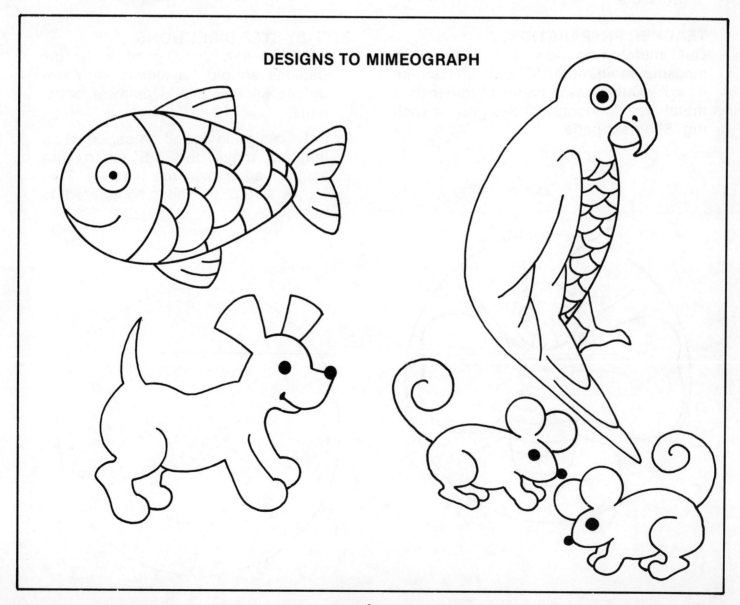

WHISTLE A HAPPY TUNE

COLLECT...
Medium weight cardboard
Scissors
Crayons

TEACHER PREPARATION...
Mimeograph whistle pattern to medium weight cardboard. Cut board to 5″ × 2″.

STEP-BY-STEP DIRECTIONS...
1. Cut out design. Fold solid center line.
2. Then fold on the dotted lines toward the center line. Cut out a small "V" in the center of the folded line.
3. Color the whistle.
4. Place tab and pointer between index finger and lips to blow.

FACE THE RULER

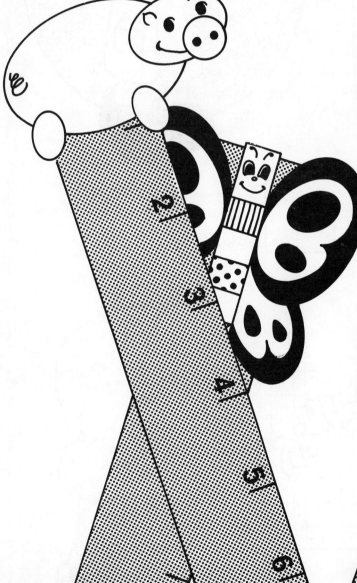

STEP-BY-STEP DIRECTIONS. . .
1. Let children select three to five maximum wood shapes. Arrange and glue shapes together to make animals, people, flowers, or objects. Concentrate on one portion of the image rather than the whole shape.

2. Let shapes dry.

3. Decorate images with acrylics and spray gloss varnish. Let dry.

4. Glue finished images to one end of ruler and let dry.

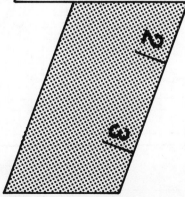

EMBROIDERED CARDS

COLLECT. . .
    Medium weight cardboard
    Needle, thread, yarn
    Scissors
    Glue

TEACHER PREPARATION. . .
Mimeograph patterns to medium weight cardboard. Establish number of cards children can make.

STEP-BY-STEP DIRECTIONS. . .
1. Instruct class to push needle in and out on the heavy black dots that form the outline of picture.
2. Long stitches go on the front side of picture; short stitches go on the back.

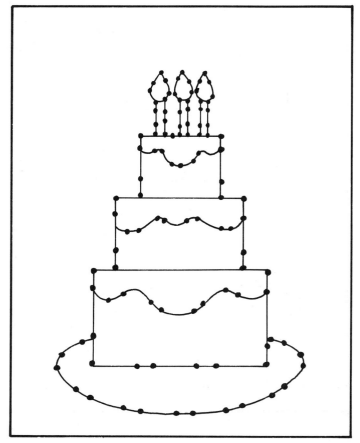

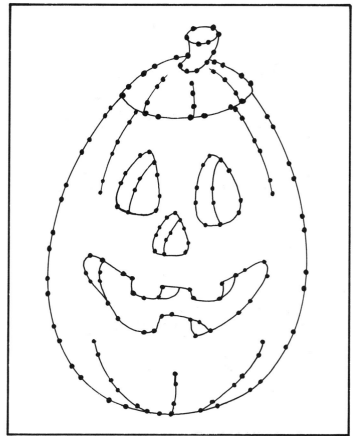

11

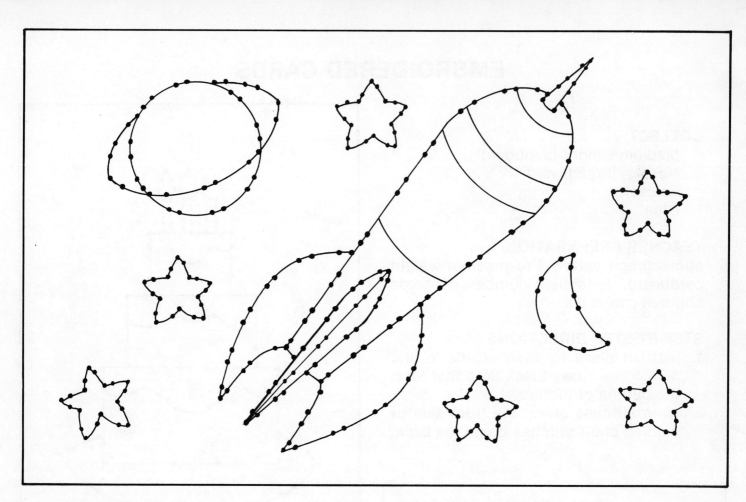

MUGS

COLLECT. . .

Clay (Schools or institutions without kilns may use AMOCO Marbelex. Marbelex is a grey clay which dries hard without firing. It is ready to use, but is not waterproof. Objects decorated with acrylic paint instead of glazes should be sprayed with clear gloss varnish to finish and seal.)
Clay tools
Glazes
Rolling pin
Slip clay
8½″ × 11″ notebook paper
Pencils
Kiln

Pinch

Coil

Slab

STEP-BY-STEP DIRECTIONS. . .

1. Roll slab ½″ thick, cut 3″ base. Then pinch, coil, or slab to make a coffee mug cylinder. Roll and attach a ¼″ thick cylinder for handle.

2. Sculpt faces, happy or sad, using above mentioned techniques. Attach features by incising surface, apply slip, and smooth rough edges. When clay is partially dry, hair, brows, and beards may be "combed" in with toothpicks, nails, etc.

3. Let dry, bisque fire in kiln, glaze, and refire. All areas of mug do not have to be glazed; teeth, eyes, and hair may be colored; inside must be glazed to waterproof. If features are not sculptured, designs may be painted with glazes.

SAND CANDLES

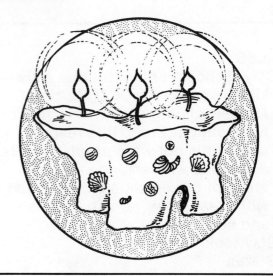

COLLECT...
- Plastic pails, boxes, milk cartons
- Damp sand
- Decorative items, such as stones, beans, peas, wood, glass, shells, etc.
- Paraffin or wax
- Cotton string 3″ longer than pail
- Stick—2″ wider than pail
- Hot plate
- Double boiler
- Candy thermometer
- Newspapers

STEP-BY-STEP DIRECTIONS...

1. Collect decorative items suggested above. In pail or container, make a shape for the candles in the damp sand. Poke holes to make legs, indentations, designs, etc. Reinforce awkward edges and shapes with newspapers. Attach decorative pieces to the sides of sand form.

2. Tie wicks at bottom, dip into melted wax, and set aside to dry. Place stick across pail and let wicks touch bottom of sand, but avoid the sides.

3. Heat wax or paraffin in top of double boiler. Use candy thermometer to check temperature: 150° yields thin sand crust; 200° yields thick sand crust. Do not reach or exceed 400° as wax may spew out of container. (Supervise melting and pouring as hot wax is dangerous.) When desired temperature is reached, pour wax into mold; do not move until completely dry.

4. Brush off excess sand. Colored wax may be poured gently over candle. Carefully remove candle from pail.

STORYBOOK BOX

COLLECT. . .
Shoe box with lid
Crayons or magic markers
Medium weight cardboard
Scissors
Glue
Drawing paper

TEACHER PREPARATION. . .
Mimeograph pattern sheets. Cut cardboard to 5″ × 7″ size. Read story of "Little Red Riding Hood" to class.

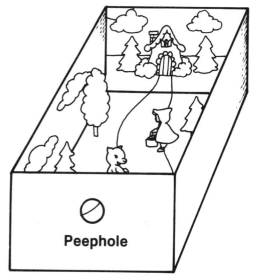

Peephole

STEP-BY-STEP DIRECTIONS. . .
1. Tell class to create grandmother's house with space between the two trees and side walk on pattern sheet. Sizes of trees and house should not exceed box height.

2. Make picture and outline with magic marker. Cut it out on markered lines and glue it inside one end of shoe box.

3. Draw trees, Riding Hood figure, and fox (see patterns on following page); glue them to medium weight cardboard. Let dry and then color.

4. Color back side of inner shoe box.

5. Decorate lid and cut out peephole.

6. Cut out shapes, gently score tabs, glue, and fold under. Apply glue to areas where figures will be placed, and attach tabs. Try this idea with other stories.

PATTERNS

STEP-BY-STEP DIRECTIONS. . .
1. Cut out patterns.
2. Glue to cardboard and dry.
3. Color and add features.
4. Score tabs.
5. Glue inside box.
6. Cut peephole, decorate lid, and cover box.

SCARY CAT, SCARY CAT...

COLLECT...
  15″ × 7″ Con-Tact paper—2 per
  child
  15″ × 7″ heavyweight cardboard—1
  per child
  Pencils
  X-acto knife
  Magic marker
  Acrylic paint
  Spray gloss varnish
  Compass
  10″ single strand fishing line or 10″
  flexible wire

TEACHER PREPARATION...
Mimeograph 8″ x 10½″ sample pattern
for children to enlarge to 14″ × 7″.

STEP-BY-STEP DIRECTIONS...
1. Tell children they are going to make a scarey cat. The hanging image of a cat is used in France to protect fruit trees and vegetable gardens from birds, rabbits, etc. It may also be used as a hanging decoration or nailed to a fence.

2. Drawing lightly in pencil, enlarge cat to 14″ × 7″ using mimeographed pattern as a guide. Outline form with magic marker. Cut out cat, using an X-acto knife. Follow cut lines indicated on pattern.

3. Lightly draw in features with pencil, using body marking pattern as a guide. Make cat as fierce and as mean as you can. Paint with acrylics and let dry. Spray with gloss varnish and let dry. Ornaments that are going to hang freely should be decorated on both sides.

4. Carefully apply Con-Tact paper to one side of animal to avoid wrinkles. Repeat on opposite side. Punch hole in middle of back with a compass, tie with fish line, or flexible wire, and hang.

5. Wind a single strand of 10″ flexible wire to cat; leave rest of wire hang so that it can be attached to a limb or fence. Knot-tie 10″ of fish line and hang to display.

ARTFUL POSTERS

COLLECT...

24" × 48" white or light blue burlap
Felt and other fabrics in variety of
  sizes and colors
Stuffing
Butcher paper
Dark blunt-point magic marker
Needles and thread, string or yarn
Glue
Scissors
1/8" or 1/2", 15" dowel rods
Decorative items: buttons, beads, se-
  quins, etc.

TEACHER PREPARATION...

Cut fabric and butcher paper into 14" ×
18" pieces.

STEP-BY-STEP DIRECTIONS...

1. Let class choose one of the following
   themes: the rainbow, hot air balloon,
   or musical symbols. Ask class what
   they associate with their choice. For
   example, balloon: clouds, colors,
   shape and design, the basket, land-
   scape.

2. Make a large, simple drawing of the
   theme with pencil on butcher paper.
   Add only a few details. (Some areas
   such as sun, clouds, or smoke may be
   raised by stuffing. Allow slightly extra
   length and width in these areas.)
   Outline pencil drawing with magic
   marker since this will serve as a pattern. Use magic markers the same colors as the fabrics.

3. Lay pattern on burlap; allow 3/4" at top for dowel rod. It may be necessary to glue or sew several pieces of fabric together to achieve a desired length or width. Let glue dry before pinning and cutting pattern.

4. Cut out shapes on magic marker lines; pin felt to fabric. Arrange items on burlap; then pin. Glue, blanket-stitch, or crossover stitch shapes on burlap. Stuff portions lightly. Then sew remaining open areas to burlap using one of the stitches named.

5. Decorative items may be added.

6. Sew 3/4" seam at top of banner and insert rod. Spot glue. Tack braided string or yarn on ends of rod. Hem bottom of banner. Poster is now ready to hang.

Crossover stitch

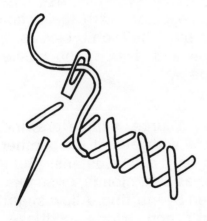

Make a series of diagonal stitches; stitch through bottom and make diagonal stitches over work.

20

MESSAGE BANNERS

COLLECT...
- 15″ × 27″ burlap
- 15″ × 27″ drawing paper
- Felt in several colors and sizes
- Glue
- Scissors
- Yarn, thread, cord
- Needles, pins
- ½″, 15″ dowel rod—1 per child
- Magic marker
- Decorative items: sequins, rickrack, beads, ribbon, etc.

Folded fabric

Hem ½″ + 1/16″.

Cut 3″ x 3″

Hem bottom of fabric ½″.

STEP-BY-STEP DIRECTIONS...

1. Write sayings or messages on notebook paper with illustrations. For example: Good Will to Men—illustrate with doves; Peace on Earth—illustrate with angel or clasped hands; My Room—Enter at Your Own Risk—illustrate with a large "X." Other messages may be Hello, Welcome, Love Ya, etc.

2. Enlarge message and drawing to 15″ × 27″. Drawings should be large since they will be used as patterns. Outline drawing with magic marker; color with markers the same colors as the felt.

3. Fold burlap in half, carefully aligning edges. Cut a 3″ rectangle 3″ from both edges. Unfold and stitch edges of rectangle, leaving ½″ (plus 1/16″) to accommodate a dowel rod. Hem ½″ at bottom of fabric.

4. Place one letter of illustration over felt, pin, and cut out one at a time. Arrange elements of design on burlap and pin in place. When satisfied with an arrangement, glue or stitch letters to burlap. (Covers may be added over felt and attached by gluing or sewing.) Add sequins, beads, ornamental rickrack, etc.

5. Insert dowel rod, attach cord with nail, glue rod in several places and let dry. Banner is NOW READY.

MESSAGE BANNERS

COLLECT. . .
Pieces of colored fabrics
Stuffing
Needle, thread, yarn
2½″ × 3¾″ drawing paper
Pencils
Scissors
Pins
Dark color, blunt-point magic marker

TEACHER PREPARATION. . .
Cut drawing paper 3″ × 3½″. Limit length of message.

STEP-BY-STEP DIRECTIONS. . .
1. Messages should be simple as Love Ya, Welcome, Smile, Dead End, etc.

2. Draw space-filling letters on drawing paper; allow extra width and height because they will be stuffed. Outline letters with magic marker, pin pattern to two pieces of fabric and cut out.

3. Stitch fabric letters together with running stitches (a machine may be used if available); leave an opening for stuffing. Carefully fold raw edges inward, and sew with overcast stitch.

4. Sew letters together to spell message either vertically or horizontally. To make hangers, use simple plastic rings or braided yarn sewn to banners.

TELL TALE SIGNS

COLLECT...

8″ × 10″ Contrast-O plastic film
(available in art and craft supply
houses)
X-acto knives
Magic markers, crayon, or ink
Pencils
Notebook paper
8″ × 10″ drawing paper
1½″ × 2½″ black and white cardboard
Glue

STEP-BY-STEP DIRECTIONS...

1. Write the name of a pet, family member, or friend listing his likes, interests, and talents. Then on drawing paper, spell name in large block letters.

2. Draw a few simple objects inside the letters. These should suggest the likes, interests, or talents. Objects may become a part of the letters, the letter, or extend beyond its edge. (See illustration.) Draw several object-letter arrangements.

3. Color objects black. Leave white space to separate the forms.

4. Copy design lightly in pencil on the white paper which protects the black layer. Use sharp X-acto knife to cut the white protective cover, being careful not to cut the black plastic beneath. Peel off the designs. (Save cutouts as they may be used for correction.)

   Color letter designs with magic marker, crayon or ink.

5. Work may be framed with 1½″ × 1½″ × 2½″ black or white cardboard. Glue or tape frame on front side of work.

MAGIC TRIANGLES AND SQUARES

COLLECT. . .
> Light, medium, and dark construction
> paper
> Scissors
> Glue
> Ruler
> Pencils

TEACHER PREPARATION. . .
Cut paper 9″ × 12″ size; mimeograph
triangle and square patterns.

STEP-BY-STEP DIRECTIONS. . .
1. Look at a square illusion and close one
   eye. It appears to face upward to the
   left, showing the bottom.
2. It also appears to face inward.
3. Experiment by gluing light, medium,
   and dark papers to both triangle and
   square patterns.
4. Make other optical illusions using
   geometric and random shapes.

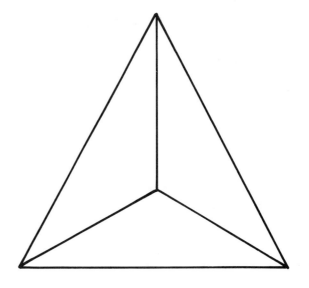

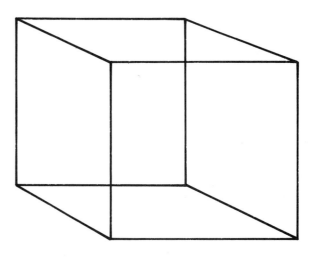

**Confused? Check
Escher and see how
he handles illusions
using animals and
geometric shapes.**

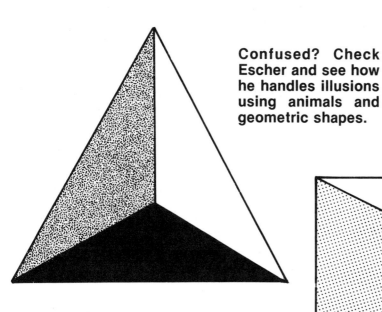

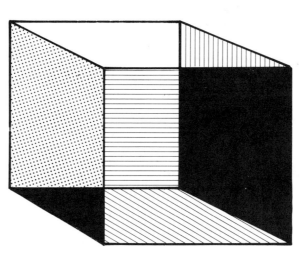

ANIMAL PROFILES

COLLECT...
  8½″ x 11″, 4″ x 6″, ½″ x 3″ x 6″, ½″
   x 3″ x 6″ oaktag paper
  Cardboard
  Glue
  Pencils
  Scissors
  Crayons
  Yarn, buttons, seeds
  Compass
  Construction paper scraps
  Paper fastener

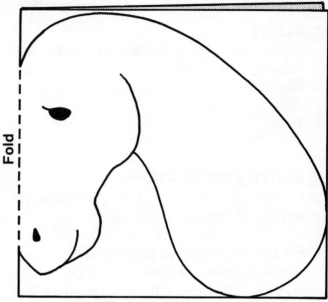

Fold

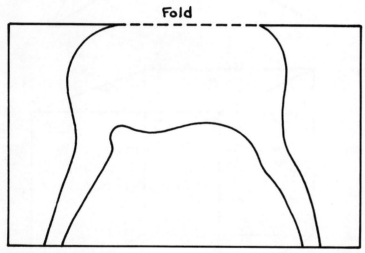

Fold

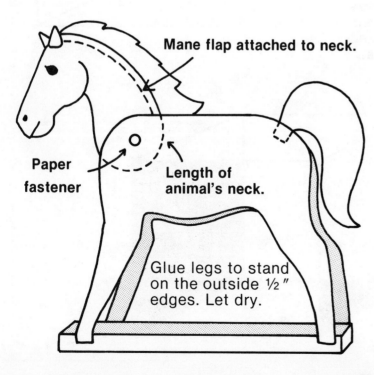

Mane flap attached to neck.

Paper fastener

Length of animal's neck.

Glue legs to stand on the outside ½″ edges. Let dry.

STEP-BY-STEP DIRECTIONS...
1. Discuss parts of animals, their basic shapes that make up their bodies, and profiles. Explain term **profile.**

2. Tell children to fold 8½″ × 11″ oaktag in half (5½″ × 11″). Draw a profile of animal along fold line. Omit face and neck. Drawing should include back, front, and rear legs, belly, and chest.

3. Fold 4″ × 6″ tag paper in half (3″ × 4″). Draw profile of animal's face on fold; rest of drawing should include chin and cheek areas. Omit ears.

4. Draw rest of the animal figures (tail, ears, manes, etc.) on single sheet of cardboard, cut out, and glue. Let dry.

5. Color animal with crayon. Add details, glue, apply construction paper ears, spots, eyes, neck and tail, hair, etc., to cardboard.

6. Make holes with compass on body in neck area; repeat on neck. Insert head; attach with paper fastener. Head should now move up and down.

7. Score ½″ x 3″ x 6″ base; color the stand with crayon. Glue pebbles, sand, etc., to top area and let dry.

OVER AND UNDER LOOSE WEAVING

COLLECT. . .
16″ × 18″ branch or stick
Yarn
Decorative items: weeds, feathers, sticks, bamboo, buttons, milkweed pods, metal nuts, etc.

STEP-BY-STEP DIRECTIONS. . .
1. Each child will need a branch or stick. Weave, braid, knot-tie, or macramé 40″ long strands of yarn.
2. Any of the decorative items may be added to work.
3. To make open areas, tie sections of warp together, and weave between and around spaces.

SLITS

STEP-BY-STEP DIRECTIONS. . .
1. Weave part of the way across the warp.
2. Go back and repeat weavings, always **stopping at the same place** to go back.
3. Repeat steps 1 and 2 on opposite side of warp.

Result: Gap or slit where weft threads meet.

Slits

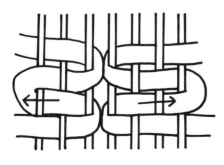

INTERLOCKING

STEP-BY-STEP DIRECTIONS. . .
1. Weave part of the way across warp on one side.
2. Repeat step 1 on opposite side.
3. **Crisscross** weft yarns over one another and weave back to edges.

Result: Slight raised surface at intersection.

Note: Both yarns must meet in same place.

Interlocking

DOVETAILING

STEP-BY-STEP DIRECTIONS. . .

1. Weave part of the way across warp. Do not loop or interlock yarns.
2. Weave to edge of warp.

   Result: Hump or ridge where yarn meets.

Dovetailing

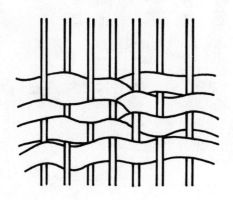

PILLOW

STEP-BY-STEP DIRECTIONS. . .

1. Sew three sides of weaving (or fabric) together.
2. Stuff with pillow foam, kapok, rags, etc.
3. Sew fourth side.
4. Fringe: Measure sample piece of desired length yarn and cut. (See illustration.) Bring folded yarn (½) through yarn on weaving or seam thread. Bring end pieces through loop.
5. Repeat step 4 until desired amount of fringe is reached.

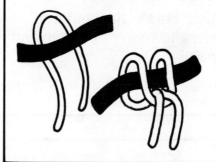

Bring ends through loop or folded yarn; pull tightly.

MACRAME

STEP-BY-STEP DIRECTIONS. . .

1. Fold yarn in half over branch or cord.
2. Bring ends through hoop of folded yarn, pull tightly, and add yarn repeating steps 1 and 2.
3. To tie half-knot or half hitch: Place right-hand cord over other three cords.
4. Pick up left-hand cord, bend it diagonally under cords and through space formed by right-hand cord, (see illustrations).
5. Repeat knotting.

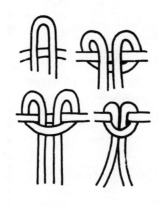
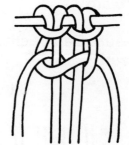
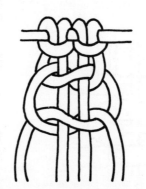

MULTI-POINTED STAR

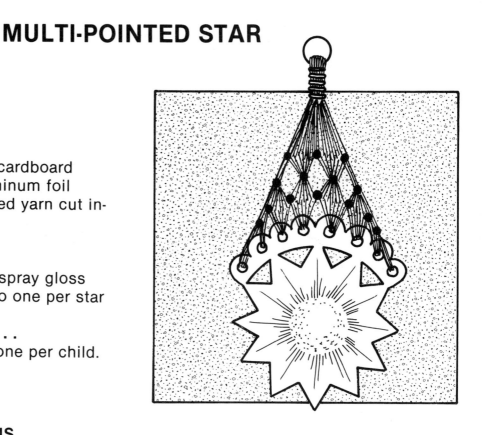

COLLECT...
Clay
Rolling pin
Tape
9" × 12" heavyweight cardboard
  tray covered with aluminum foil
1 dark and 1 light colored yarn cut into 40" lengths
1-1" metal ring
Kiln
Glazes or acrylics with spray gloss
  varnish—limit colors to one per star

TEACHER PREPARATION...
Mimeograph clay pattern, one per child.

STEP-BY-STEP DIRECTIONS...
1. Roll ¼" clay slab on cardboard tray. Lightly scratch star outline on clay. Cut out pattern and lay on clay for basic outline.
2. Punch 1/8" or slightly larger holes to allow for shrinkage and insertion of yarn. Remove excess clay.

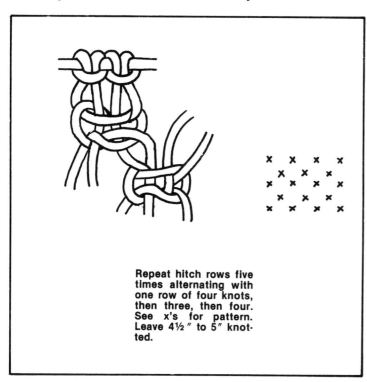

Repeat hitch rows five times alternating with one row of four knots, then three, then four. See x's for pattern. Leave 4½" to 5" knotted.

3. Lightly scratch divisions for decorating star with repeating geometric or random designs. Clay may be decorated with scratch-in lines with punctures made by pins, combs, nails, pencils, textures, fabric impressions. Small individual balls may be made, attached to clay, and then punched with a nail head.
4. Let clay dry, fire, glaze and refire or paint with a spray gloss varnish finish.
5. Tape finished star to desk and thread yarn through loops. Alternate one dark yarn and one light color in loops. Macramé yarns using the half-knot and half hitch. Small wood beads may be added for decoration.
6. Wrap yarn around ring. Take 10" piece of yarn and, holding one end in finger, wrap all ends of the macramé yarns and the piece that will then be wound around threads. Loosely wrap three windings, and insert end of thread. Pull excess until taut. Secure with glue to prevent it from coming untied.

29

PATTERN—POINTED STAR

HIEROGLYPHIC NAME PLATE

COLLECT. . .
Clay
Clay tools
Rolling pin
18″ × 20″ aluminum foil-covered
   cardboard tray
Glazes (limit choice of 3)
Acrylic paint and spray gloss varnish
   (limit color to 3)
Heavy string or cord

TEACHER PREPARATION. . .
Mimeograph letters with accompanying
symbols and space to write and draw
name with hieroglyphs.

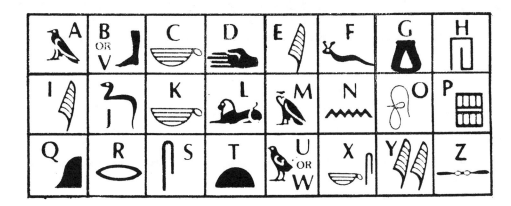

STEP-BY-STEP DIRECTIONS. . .

1. In ancient times, royalty had their names made in oval pendants to wear as a symbol of their royalty or their individual mark.

2. Print first, middle, and/or last names (avoid nicknames) in the boxes. Draw related symbols.

3. Roll clay into ½″ length to be determined by individual's name. On clay, carve name with symbols by using incising, coil, or slab techniques. Attach symbols by scratching surface, affixing coil or slab, and smoothening surrounding clay. Attach two coils to top or back of plaque for hanging.

4. Let dry, bisque fire, glaze and refire, or paint with acrylics and spray with gloss varnish. Let dry.

5. Attach and knot cord to clay coils for hanging; puncture slabs, add knotted cord and hang.

NOTE: Cardboard may be used in place of clay to make name tags.

HIEROGLYPHIC GUIDE

Name: _____

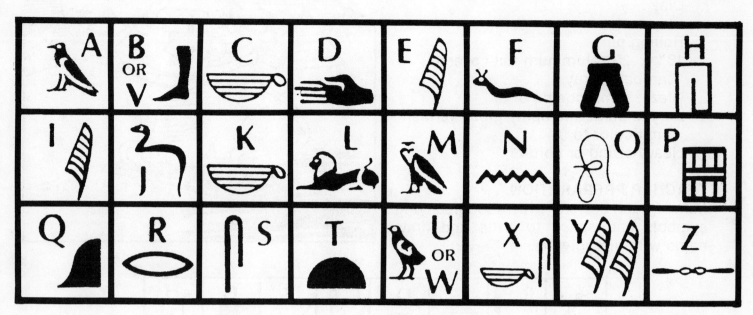

Practice making your name, parents, friends, etc., using hieroglph symbols.

NAME	HIEROGLYPH

CEREALIZED SCHOOL BUS

COLLECT. . .

Oatmeal or cornmeal boxes (1 per child)
Two spools
Two short pencils
White and colored construction paper
Glue
Magic marker
Pencils
X-acto knives
Black and white acrylic paint
Compass

STEP-BY-STEP DIRECTIONS. . .

1. Cut colored construction paper to exact length to go around box once. Leave top off and glue paper around box.

2. Make wheel holes: Cut two square holes, one toward the front and the other toward the rear with an X-acto knife.

3. Paint spools black; paint hub caps white.

4. Punch axle holes with compass point through the box above wheel holes. Now push axles (short pencil) through one of the holes. Repeat for second axle.

5. Make bottom of box the rear window and the top the front of the bus. Cut 2″ × (length of box) drawing paper.

6. Draw with pencil five or more rectangles for windows and place heads of riders in each.

7. Draw large rectangles for back windows (the bottom) and front (the top).

8. Draw back views of heads and benches on the back rectangle.

9. On the front, draw driver behind wheel. Cut out circles for headlights. Glue in place.

10. Color figures with magic marker or crayon. Print identification on white drawing paper. Cut to fit side of bus and glue on side of the bus.

11. Cut and glue in front and rear of bus bumpers.

Front

Rear

Front and rear lights

License plates

Side Windows

Bus, name, school district, etc.

HANGING BLOCK NAMES

COLLECT. . .
Clay
Clay tools
Rolling pin
String or yarn
Metal ring

TEACHER PREPARATION. . .
Mimeograph block letter style sheet.

STEP-BY-STEP DIRECTIONS. . .

1. Roll clay ½" × 3" to make letters of children's names. Use letter style sheet as a guide to cut letters. Punch one hole at the top and one at the bottom of each letter. Let dry, bisque fire, glaze, and refire letters. Paint with acrylics, if not glazing, and spray varnish when finished; let dry.

2. Start with last letter of name; thread yarn through hole at the top and through hole at the bottom of next letter. Tie yarn and continue tying rest of letters to spell name. Then tie a bow through top hole of last letter, and fasten yarn by wrapping around and tying it to a metal ring. Names are ready to be hung.

BLOCK LETTER GUIDE

Name: _____

A B C D E

F G H I J

K L M N O

P Q R S T

U V W X Y

Z

NOTE TO TEACHER. . .
Felt may be substituted for clay. Cut two
pieces, sew together with blanket or running stitches and lightly stuff.

LANTERN HOUSE

COLLECT. . .
- Clay
- Rolling pin
- Clay tools
- Slip clay
- Votive candleholder and candle
- Newspaper
- 8″ × 8″ aluminum-covered cardboard tray

NOTE TO TEACHER. . .
Black areas are cut out for light to show.

Roof

Side Walls

Dormer Side Walls
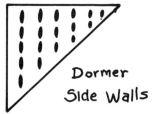

Dormer Roof

Dormer Front Wall
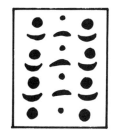

Chimney

Front and Back Walls

STEP-BY-STEP DIRECTIONS. . .

1. Roll four slabs of clay to uniform ½″ thickness. Use a ruler and clay tools, cut slabs to 6″ × 4″. Punch holes in walls with pencils, pen caps, knives, or spools. Let walls dry slightly.

2. Roll two 5″ × 5″ × ½″ slabs of clay for roof and punch openings to let light shine through. Let dry slightly. Roll ½″ slabs of different heights for dormers and chimneys. Let clay dry slightly before pinching two walls together. Place crumpled newspapers (it will burn out during firing) inside dormer and chimney walls for support.

3. Pinch two walls together at a time. Pinch roof together and attach dormers. Place newspapers inside house walls for support. Pinch to attach roof to walls; pinch to attach chimney to walls.

37

4. Roll clay 7″ × 7″ × ½″ for base. DO NOT ATTACH TO HOUSE. To form a holder for candle, press candleholder into center of base. Enlarge depression slightly to allow for shrinkage. When dry, remove excess clay around the edges.

5. Bisque fire, glaze, and refire. (If not glazing, paint with acrylics and spray with gloss varnish to finish. Paint with flame-resistant material.)

6. Place candleholder with candle in depression in base. Light it and lower house onto base.

WATERCOLOR MOSAICS, ETC.

COLLECT. . .
    Cardboard cut into different sizes
    Watercolor containers
    Glue

STEP-BY-STEP DIRECTIONS. . .
1. Arrange and glue empty watercolor containers to board.
2. Containers may be reversed or color side up.

WEED OR PENCIL HOLDERS: Form clay into a ball and use pencils or small finger to poke holes of various depths and sizes. Fire in kiln. (Glazing and refiring are optional.) Holders may be decorated with acrylic paints and gloss varnished.

STYROFOAM CREATURES: Collect sheets of styrofoam used for packing. Fasten styrofoam with glue, tape, or string to create people, animals, or objects. Creatures may be painted, then decorated with peas, beans, buttons, yarn, cloth, etc.

APPLE HEADS: Peel an unbruised apple. Then carve a face. Exaggerate features as nose, eyes, ears, etc. Soak apple thirty minutes in vinegar. Place on a tray to dry, allowing space between. Collect and cut sticks approximately 8″. Sharpen one end to a point. Carefully puncture bottom through core with the stick. Costumes may be made or work may be glued to a decorated tin can.

DECOUPAGE: Carefully cut out pictures and arrange on board or foil pans. Pictures may be overlapped. Glue in place; wipe away excess. Apply many layers of Mod-Podge (a commercial product) or lacquer. Let dry between applications.

NECKLACES: Five quarts of popped corn, needle, string, scissors, spray paint. Spray paint popped corn. Then string on lengths 8″, 10″, 14″, and 18″ of thread to make necklaces. Necklaces may be of one or more strands. If it is a holiday season, experiment with snow, glitter and other combinations. String beads separately or in combination with popcorn. Make necklaces of styrofoam packing "peanuts."

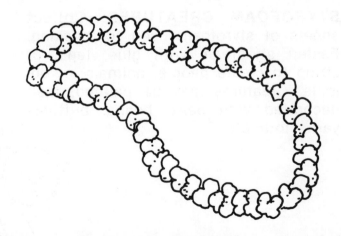

STUFFED CUDDLIES

COLLECT. . .

Polyester filling
Felt scraps
Needle
Thread, yarn
Straight pins
Scissors
Decorations: wiggle eyes, buttons,
 beads, ribbon
Glue
Drawing paper, pencils
Crayons, magic marker

TEACHER PREPARATION. . .

Cut felt and drawing paper into 4″ x 5″ pieces. Mimeograph pattern furnished, if children do not create their own.

STEP-BY-STEP DIRECTIONS. . .

1. To make patterns, sketch large simple animals, such as dogs, cats, pigs, fish, etc., on drawing paper.

2. Outline sketches with crayon or magic marker.

3. Pin sketches to two pieces of felt; cut out on outlines through all thicknesses.

4. Remove pattern.

5. Repeat steps 2, 3 and 4 for fins, ears, feathers, octopus legs—be sure you have 8.

6. Sew with running stitch halfway around form; then stuff. Stitch opening closed.

7. Backstitch last stitch; snip excess thread or yarn.

8. Sew or glue eyes, noses, mouths, etc., to pets. Let dry.

9. Pets may be wrapped for gift giving.

PATTERNS

BIBLIOGRAPHY

Eisner, Elliot W. *Educating Artistic Vision.* New York: Macmillan Company, 1972.

Harvey, Virginia L. *Macramé: The Art of Creative Knotting.* New York: Van Nostrand Reinhold Company, 1967.

Lowenfeld, Viktor, and Lambert W. Britain. *Creative and Mental Growth.* London: Macmillan Company, 1982.

Mayer, Ralph. *The Artists Handbook on Materials and Techniques.* New York: The Viking Press, 1981.

Rainey, Sarita R. *Weaving Without a Loom.* New York: Prentice-Hall, 1977.